The Sweeet Old Lady Coloring and Activity Book.

By Catherine D. Killam
Art by Richard Svensson

Acknowledgments

I wish to thank my beloved husband, Kent, who has supported me in all that I've wanted to do and has been there helping make so many of my dreams come true.

Thank you to Lynn Morrison for her suggestions and her encouragement from the first moment I mentioned writing this book. To my daughter, Kristin, for her encouragement and support. Thank you to my daughter-in-law, Lenae, Marie Stumpf and Ira Ono for their really helpful suggestions. I am also grateful to Joanna Devoe, my YouTube friend, who inspires and motivates me with her upbeat and "can do" attitude.

A big thank you to Richard Svensson whose talent and imagination brought "The Sweeet Old Lady" to life. A big thank you to Koli Cutler for his audio and American Sign Language skills. I feel so lucky to have found you. Thank you to Kay and Carter Sams of SisterPixel for the use of their clip art image of the purple pointy hat. Please visit them at
www.etsy.com/shop/SisterPixel.

Thank you to Decy Devere and Norma Beuschel for their support of Cat-Care. My gratitude also to Boyd Castro, DVM, and his wife, Ann, of Hilo Veterinary Clinic LLC, for their assistance with the cats through all the years.

I would also like to thank my son, Jason, and daughter-in-law, Lenae, for bringing Jayln and Kaylee, my twin granddaughters, into this world. The girls motivated me to want to write a children's book.

Dedication:

To Norma Beuschel
I am grateful for her support of
Cat-Care through the years.
I know "kitty loving time"
made a deep impression on her
and she has made a
deep impression on me.

All the author's net proceeds
from the sale of this book are
donated to Cat-Care,
a 501(c)3 nonprofit,
cat rescue and sanctuary
for abandoned kittens and cats.

Please see the last page of this
book for life saving tips
for pets.

There is a sweet old lady
down the street,
the kind of lady you really should meet.
She lives in a red and white
gingerbread house
in an enchanted forest with
her gnome-looking spouse.
The roof is the color of chocolate brown.
It is the cutest house in all of the town.
The moss makes a luxurious
carpet of green
and with the tall trees,
it is a magical scene.

Her face is friendly and full of wrinkles
and her eyes are always full of twinkles.
You know she is exceedingly wise
when you look carefully into her eyes.
She smells of lavender, lilac or rose
from the top of her head
right down to her toes.
Her hair is becoming very gray.
That's fine because she likes it that way.
Sometimes she wears her hair
up in a bun.
Sometimes she wears it down
just for fun.
She's the sweet old lady down the street.

She likes to wear long purple dresses
and threads all sorts of
flowers in her tresses.
She loves going out in funky shoes
and sporting various crazy hairdos.
She has a selection of pointy hats
and beautiful earrings shaped like cats.
She always walks with a dancer's grace
and is never seen without a smile on her face.
This lovely lady is even kind to rats
and she often enjoys dancing with cats.
Her voice is bright and full of glee
and she would never even harm a flea.
She's the sweet old lady down the street.

She gets up early, before the
crack of dawn
and sits outside on the
backyard lawn.
She likes to pray and meditate;
it puts her in a peaceful state.
She listens to the hum
of the bees and the flowers.
Oh, how she loves these morning hours.
She says her secret to a happy life
is not to fill it with anger and strife.
She tries to never ever judge
and to never ever hold a grudge.
She's the sweet old lady down the street.

She wears red sneakers with her
purple jogging suit.
Her cat helps motivate her
with a carrot root.
She eats healthy food and
she loves to exercise.
She knows that good health
is the ultimate prize;
and too many treats will go to her thighs.
After her run,
she'll take a short break,
then make herself a healthy
green protein shake.
She's the sweet old lady down the street.

She has a house just for cats
with special fluffy welcoming mats.
Lots of these cats were
abandoned or strays
who didn't have any food for days.
Some cats were scared and skinny
and came from the dump.
Now they have a home
and they are happy and plump.
Oh, it's so much fun
when she rings the chime
and all the cats run to her for
"kitty loving time."
She's the sweet old lady down the street.

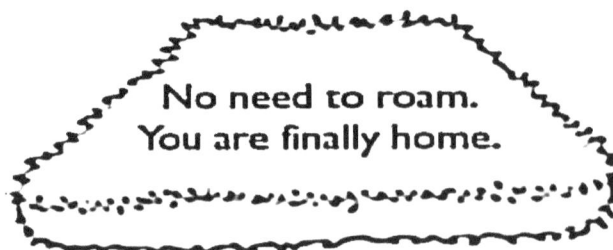

No need to roam.
You are finally home.

She feeds lots of hungry or sad looking dogs
and even takes care of little green frogs.
All her pets have a microchip.
She knows this very important tip.
If one of her micro-chipped pets
became lost, it will help them
get home for a very small cost.
She makes sure they have a collar and tag,
and that really makes their tails wag.
The sweet old lady has fairies in her yard
and she talks poetically, like a bard.
You'll often hear her speak in rhyme,
but just occasionally, not all of the time.
She's the sweet old lady down the street.

Please call
Sweeet Old Lady
555-LOVE

ye meal is served

She has a cupboard
full of enchanting herbs
and she speaks gently
with loving words.
She makes all sorts of tasty dishes
filled with love
and special wishes.
She adds delicious flavors and spice
to make everything delightful and nice.
She has a kind and giving heart
and she makes the very
best strawberry tart.
She's the sweet old lady down the street.

She drinks reviving herbal teas
under a beautiful canopy of trees.
She makes a scrumptious
soup of nettle
outside in a very large copper kettle.
She knows which plants
cure sniffles and ills
so she makes them
into healthy meals.
So if you are one of the hungry or poor
she'll give you some soup
if you come to her door.
She's the sweet old lady down the street.

She must have green thumbs
and magical powers
because her garden is
full of beautiful flowers.
She smells the flowers
after the rain showers.
She says it's a wonderful way
to spend the afternoon hours.
She asks each plant and flower
to tell her of their healing power.
She even talks to the bugs and bees
and you will often see her hug the trees.
Her garden has all the colors of the rainbow
which forms the bridge her animals will follow.
She's the sweet old lady down the street.

She studies the phases
of the moon
to know when to plant
and when to prune.
She loves to dance
to her favorite tune
under the Strawberry Moon, in June.
She'll get so dizzy
she will even swoon.
She loves to watch the stars
float across the sky.
She'll get so deeply moved, she'll even cry.
She's the sweet old lady down the street.

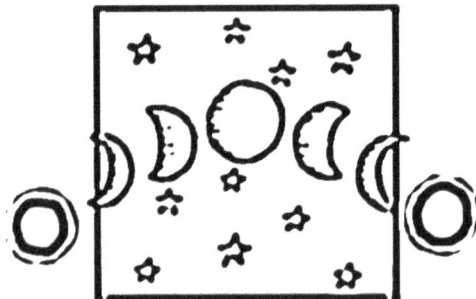

She celebrates the four seasons as they go by.
She even celebrates the fourth of July.
She sings to the stars, sun and moon
a little chant or a pretty tune.
She also honors mother earth
sometimes with reverence,
sometimes with mirth.
She knows the precious gift of each new day
and tries to honor it in every way.
She knows what she does for others
returns to her, times three.
When she says "Goodbye" she always
adds "Blessed Be."
She's the sweet old lady down the street.

Now don't think because
she is old and sweet
that she is either timid or weak.
Oh, no, that would be absolutely wrong.
This old lady is
bold, courageous and strong.
Nobody tells her what to think or to do.
She knows who she is and
to her heart she is true.
If you come to their house on Halloween,
she and her spouse
will give you jelly beans.
She's the sweet old lady down the street.

She has a magical room
filled with crystals and gems,
phenomenal books and feather pens.
She plays with funny-looking cards
and she studies the mysteries of the stars.
She also knows the art
of making a natal chart.
She makes a soothing healing potion of
rose hip oil and lavender lotion.
She also makes a magical ink
and homemade candles
of green and pink.
She's the sweet old lady down the street.

She believes in letting positive energy flow
and she's helped more animals
than we'll ever know.
She's trained in many a healing art
and she gives freely from her pure heart.
She wears a purple bracelet
with a very special charm.
It reminds her,
"Above all else, do no harm."
She firmly believes that angels are real
and they are the ones who help her heal.
She has a gentle and loving touch
and she enjoys helping others so very much.
She's the sweet old lady down the street.

GET WELL SOON
Missing you

You've met the old lady
who lives down the street
and now you know why
people have nicknamed her
"Sweeet."
You don't have to be old to be sweet.
Anyone can be sweet
and that's really neat!
So if you ever wonder how to respond
when you're in a stew
just ask yourself,
"What would the Sweeet Old Lady do?"
Then you can become a "Sweeetie," too!
She's "The Sweeet Old Lady Down the Street."

The Sweeet Old Lady is very concerned about animals.
She makes sure all of her cats and dogs wear a collar and tag
and have been microchipped. A microchip is a small metal piece about the size of a
grain of rice that is inserted under the skin on the back of the neck of a dog or
cat by a veterinarian. It has a special number that is assigned to the pet's guardian
which will have information such as the guardian's name, address, and phone number.

Please ask your parents if your pets have a microchip.
If your pets don't have a microchip, please talk to your parents about microchips.
Please make sure your pet(s) have a collar and tag
with your family's name and phone number on the tag.
Maybe it can be your job to remind your parent(s) or guardian that
your pet(s) need to wear a collar and tag and have a microchip.
You might offer to do chores to earn money to buy the microchip, collar and tag.

Here's a rhyme to help you remember
to always have your pets wear a collar and tag.

Collar and tag. Collar and tag.
All cats and dogs need a collar and tag!
Collar and tag. Collar and tag.
Here's another tip. They also need a microchip!
Collar and tag. Collar and tag.
Add your id on their tag and their tails will really wag!
Collar and Tag. Collar and Tag.

How to become a Sweeetie.

Sweeetie

If you would like to become a "Sweeetie", just color all the pages in this book and complete all the activities on the following pages.

You will learn about kindness, compassion, empathy and gratitude. You will also learn the importance of pets wearing a collar and tag with identification and also having a microchip.

You will show that you really care about animals.

After you have finished the book, have an adult verify that you have completed all the pages and reviewed all the answers with you.
The adult can then sign the
"Sweeetie Certificate" at the end of the book.
You will then become a "Sweeetie".

Color all the things a responsible Pet Guardian needs to provide for their dogs.

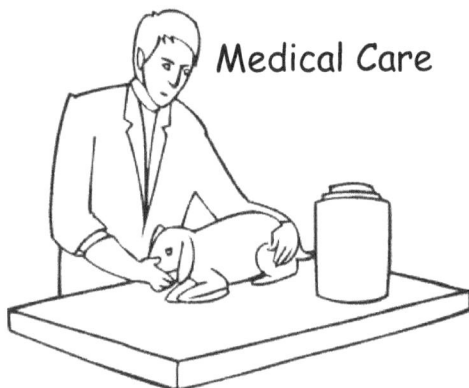

Fresh Clean Water

Food

Shelter

Medical Care

Training

Grooming

Playtime, exercise and toys.

Collar and tag with guardian's name & phone number. Microchip.

Sweet Lady
555-1234

Lots of Love!

Did you know cats need the same things as dogs?
They need water, food, shelter, medical care, training, grooming,
playtime, exercise, toys, collar & tag with id, microchip and most importantly LOVE!
Because cats like to climb they need a special break-away collar that is made
just for them. Remember to replace their collar if they should lose it.

See Answers Page 38

All cats are special and different, even if they look the same.
Can you spot the difference in these cats?
Which cat is different from the other three cats.
Circle the letter of the cat that is different.

A.

B.

C.

D.

See Answers
Page 39

Can you see what is missing on these dogs?
They all need a collar and tag so that if they get lost
people who find them can help them get home.
When dogs are outside and not on their own property
they also need to be on a leash.
Please colors the dogs then give them a collar, tag and leash.

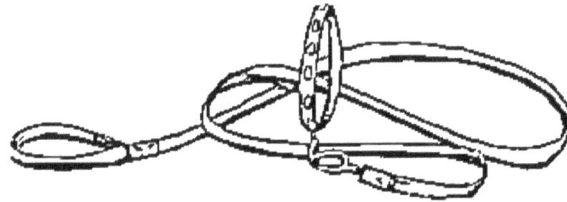

See Answers
Page 40

This poor kitty is lost and wants to go home.
If he had a collar and tag with his guardian's name and
phone number on the tag, anyone who found him could
help him get home. Because he has no identification,
he must try to get home on his own.
Can you show him the way?
Draw a line to his home.

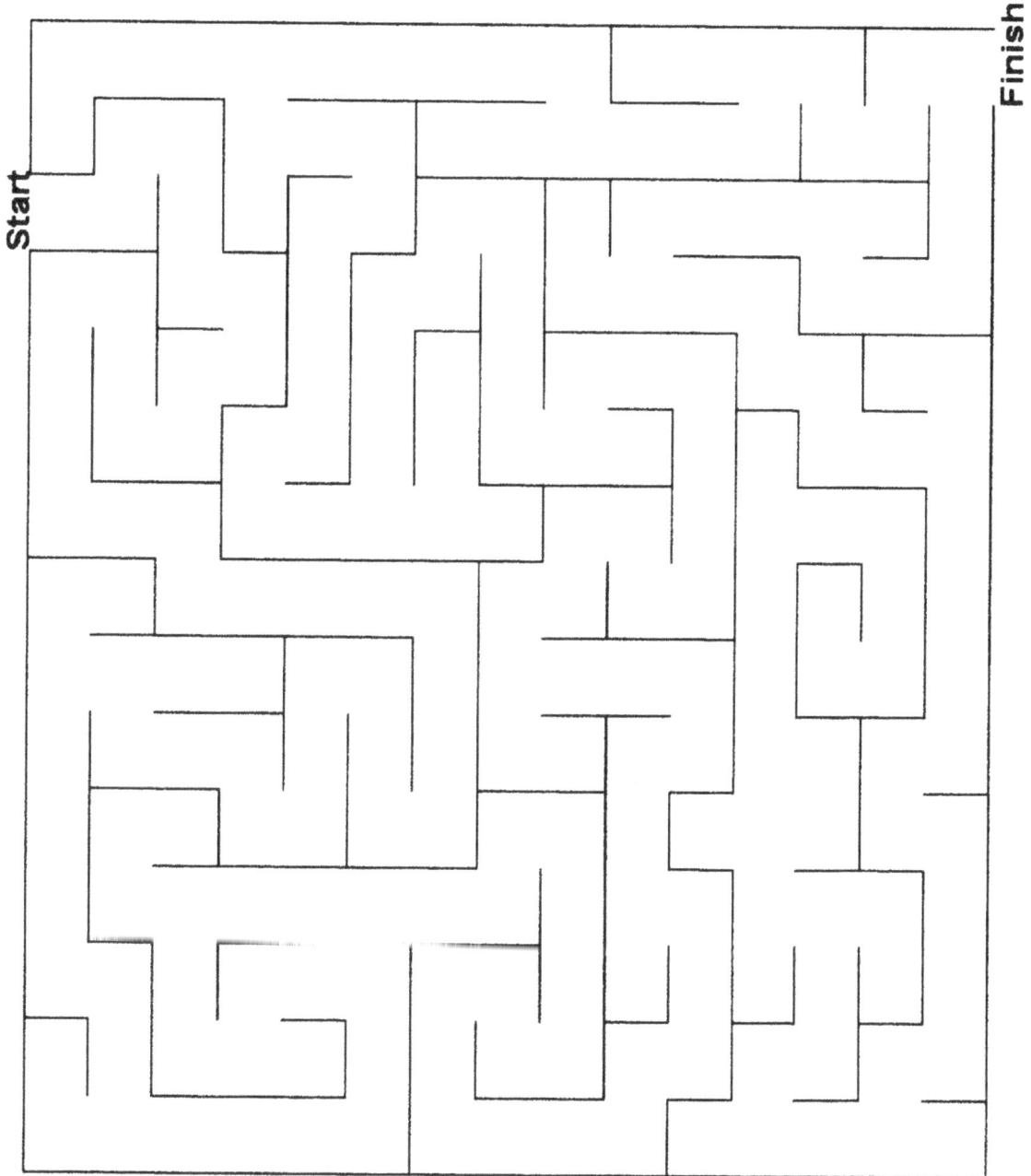

Start

Finish

See Answers
Page 41

Learning about a microchip for your pet.

1. What is a microchip for your pet?
   a. It is a special collar that the animal wears.
   b. It is a small metal piece inserted under the animal's skin behind it's neck.
   c. It is a tattoo that is placed in the animal's ear.
   d. It is a crystal attached to the animal's collar.

2. What is the approximate size of a microchip?
   a. It is about the size of a grain of rice.
   b. It is about the size of a ping pong ball.
   c. It is about the size of your thumb.
   d. It is about the size of a pencil.

3. Where do you buy a microchip for your pet?
   a. The grocery store.
   b. The pet store.
   c. The veterinarian.
   d. School.

4. What does a microchip have written on it?
   a. A special number which refers back to the guardian's name, address and phone number.
   b. The pet's name.
   c. The pet guardian's name and phone number.
   d. The animal's favorite food.

5. Why is a microchip important?
   a. They cost a lot of money.
   b. Because microchips come from the moon.
   c. Because a microchip looks like a diamond.
   d. It will identify the pet's guardian should the pet get lost.

Which picture below do you think is a pet microchip? _____

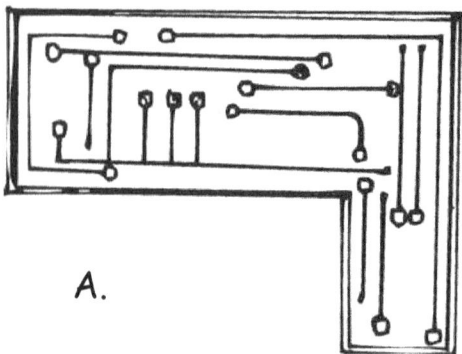

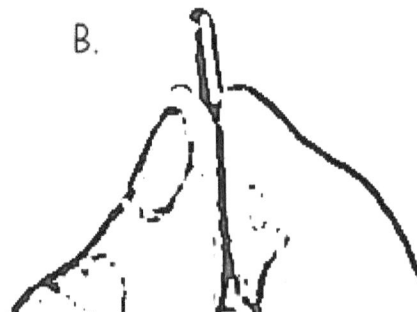

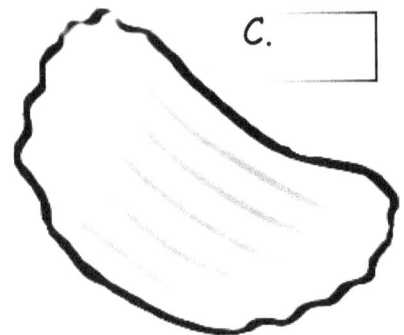

A.

B.

C.

See Answers
Page 42

Family Activity

Do you know what the words kindness, empathy and compassion mean?
Talk with your family and ask them
for examples of kindness, empathy and compassion.

Kindness means being friendly, generous and considerate.
For example: Your friend doesn't have any toys and you give your friend
one of your toys so they will also have a toy.
Can you think of an another example of kindness?

_____

_____

How could someone be kind to you?

_____

_____

Empathy means to understand and feel what someone else is feeling.
For example: A member of your family or a friend is sad because they lost
something they loved. You would understand how they feel because you
know how you would feel if you lost something you loved.
Can you think of an another example of empathy?

_____

_____

How could someone have empathy for you?

_____

_____

Compassion means to care about others and wanting to help
them if they are sick, hungry, or in need of help.
For example: A person or animal is very hungry because they have no food.
A compassionate person might give them food or volunteer
their time or money to an organization that provides food for them.
Can you think of an another example of compassion?

_____

_____

How could someone show compassion for you?

_____

_____

See Answers
Page 43

Color the lady feeding the cats.
Then unscramble the following letters to find the words
COMPASSION, EMPATHY, KINDNESS, GRATITUDE

E S N S I K D

_ _ _ _ _ _ _ _

S I N O P S O C M A

_ _ _ _ _ _ _ _ _ _

R T G A U T E D I

_ _ _ _ _ _ _ _ _

A H Y E P M T

_ _ _ _ _ _ _

See Answers
Page 44

The Sweeet Old Lady has an attitude of gratitude.
She makes a Gratitude List once a year on her birthday.
Gratitude means to be thankful for or appreciate and acknowledge
a benefit or blessing that one has received.
For example: good health, a loving family, a home, food.
Write down 12 things that you are grateful or thankful for now.
Today's date _____

1. _____

2. _____

3. _____

4. _____

5. _____

6. _____

7. _____

8. _____

9. _____

10. _____

11. _____

12. _____

It would be nice to write a Gratitude List each year.
Choose a time such as your birthday or Thanksgiving
to write another Gratitude List.
There are additional pages at the end of the book you can use.
If you keep this book, you can compare your lists over the years.

There are no right or
wrong answers.
See Page 45

There is a kind message hidden below.
Circle the words that are in the
same style as *kind*.
Write the words on the line below.

Collar DOGS *to*

gratitude compassion

kind Exercise the *on*

Grooming Tag

BIRDS Be

and FROGS Food *at*

each Love

Shelter CATS

animals Micro-chip empathy

kindness

FISH

__ __/__ __ __ __ __/__ __/__ __ __ __ __ __ __ __.

See Answers Page 46

Color the groundhog then unscramble the letters to see what good morning message he has for you.

I S R E   D N A   N I S E H

____ ___ _____.

See Answers
Page 47

The Sweeet Old Lady likes to drink herbal teas
from her pretty teapot.
Can you find the one teapot that is different
from the other three teapots.

A.

B.

C.

D.

Write the letter of the picture that is different. _____

See Answers
Page 48

The Sweeet Old lady studies the phases of the moon
so she will know when to plant and when to prune.
She also loves to dance under the Strawberry Moon in June.

Moon Cycles

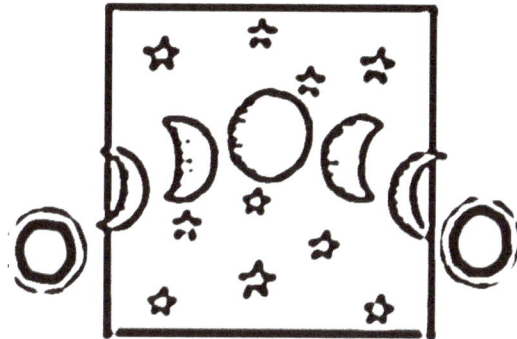

New, Waxing, Full, Waning, Dark
Waxing means to get bigger. Waning means to get smaller.

Y R R E B W A R T S
E L D Y L R J L Z L
N L W A N I N G W G
U U N W T N N A B R
R F E N D J X R W L
P N A A X I U L Y Y
D L R Y N M J N D Y
P K R G D D P Y E M

Can you find and circle the following words?
NEW, WAXING, FULL, WANING, DARK,
STRAWBERRY, PLANT, PRUNE, JUNE

See Answers
Page 49

You've met the Sweeet Old Lady Down the Street.
Let's see how much you remember about the story.

Circle the correct answer.

1. Where does the sweeet old lady down the street live?
   a. She lives in a seashell under the sea.
   b. She lives in a shoe with lots of children.
   c. She lives in a red and white gingerbread house.
   d. She lives in a castle in the clouds.

2. Why do all of her pets have a microchip?
   a. If they get hungry, they can have a snack.
   b. If they get lost, it will help them get home if someone finds them.
   c. It is a good-looking gem on their collar.
   d. It helps them see in the dark.

3. What is true about the sweeet old lady?
   a. She dances under the Harvest Moon in October.
   b. She is also known as Mrs. Claus.
   c. She eats healthy food and loves to exercise.
   d. She goes to bed late and wakes up for lunch.

4. How does the sweeet old lady show kindness, compassion and empathy?
   a. She feeds the hungry and poor.
   b. She provides a home for abandoned and stray cats.
   c. She feeds lots of hungry or sad looking dogs.
   d. All of the above.

5. What best describes the structure of the story?
   a. The story tells who the sweeet old lady is and what she does.
   b. The story is a mystery about when the sweeet old lady disappeared.
   c. The story is a play in which there is a part for each speaker even the sweeet old lady.
   d. The story is science fiction and its surroundings is set in the future.

6. Who is most likely the narrator of this story?
   a. The husband of the Sweeet Old Lady.
   b. The Sweeet Old Lady.
   c. A person who lives up the street from the sweeet old lady.
   d. A person who lives down the street from the sweeet old lady.

7. According to the illustrations, what would be the Sweeet Old Lady's favorite color?
   a. black
   b. purple
   c. pink
   d. green

See Answers
Page 50

8. Why does the Sweeet Old Lady like to pray and meditate?
   a. It helps her plan so she won't be late.
   b. It puts her in a peaceful state.
   c. It gets her ready for her date.
   d. It relaxes her stomach from what she ate.

9. What does her doormat say?
   a. "No trespassing."
   b. "The Sweeet Old Lady Lives Here."
   c, "No need to roam, You are finally home."
   d. "Welcome."

10. What is the best dish she makes?
    a. nettle soup
    b. strawberry tart
    c. chocolate cake
    d. cherry pie

11. What does she and her spouse hand out for Halloween?
    a. green protein shakes
    b. sugar cookies
    c. jelly beans
    d. chocolate bars

12. What is on her earrings?
    a. shiny stars
    b. purple flowers
    c. golden cats
    d. golden dogs

13. What does it mean to have "green thumbs"?
    a. To have green paint on the thumbs.
    b. To be born with thumbs that are green.
    c. To be awarded with the Green Thumbs prize for recycling.
    d. To be good at gardening and growing flowers.

14. What does the Sweeet Old Lady also say every time she says "Goodbye"?
    a. "See you later alligator."
    b. "Adios."
    c. "Aloha."
    d. "Blessed Be."

15. Why does the Sweeet Old Lady study the phases of the moon?
    a. To know when it's night and when it's noon.
    b. To know when the plant and when to prune.
    c. To know how many more days until the month of June.
    d. To know that her bedtime is coming soon.

See Answers
Page 51

True or False   Put a "T" if the statement is true.
Put an "F" if the statement is false.

____ 1. The sweeet old lady lives in an enchanted forest.

____ 2. The sweeet old lady makes a Gratitude List once a year on Thanksgiving.

____ 3. The sweeet old lady only wears her hair in a bun.

____ 4. The sweeet old lady has cats, but no dogs.

____ 5. The sweeet old lady makes tasty dishes filled with love and special wishes.

____ 6. The sweeet old lady drinks coffee in the woods.

____ 7. The sweeet old lady feeds hungry or poor people.

____ 8. The sweeet old lady microchips all her pets.

____ 9. The sweeet old lady doesn't like frogs.

____ 10. The sweeet old lady isn't married and lives alone.

What four things do your cat or dog need that will help them get home if they ever get lost.

1. _____

2._____

3. _____

4. _____

What do dogs and cats need lots of? ____ ____ ____ ____

See Answers
Page 52

If you colored all the pages and completed all the activities in this book,
it is now time to check your answers on the following page.

After you have reviewed all your answers with an adult,
have them sign the
"Sweeetie Certificate".
You will then become a "Sweeetie".

You have learned about compassion, kindness, and empathy.
You also learned about gratitude and made a gratitude list.
You know the importance of pets wearing a collar and tag
with identification and you also know about microchips.

Thank you for caring about animals.

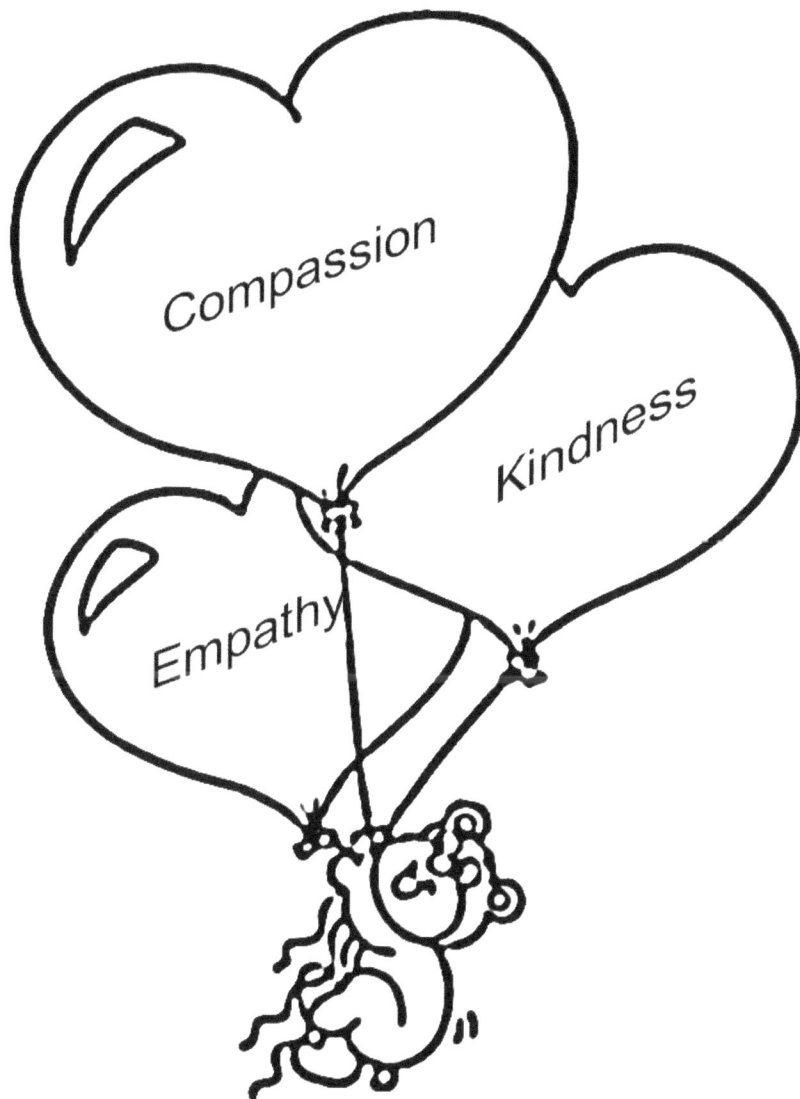

Compassion

Kindness

Empathy

Answers to Questions

Page 38 - Did you color all the items a dog or cat needs?

Page 39 - B.

Page 40 - Do all the dogs have collars, tags and leashes?

Page 42 - 1 b, 2 a, 3 c, 4 c, 5 d and the picture is B.

Page 43 - Share your answers to all the questions with an adult. Did you talk about the meanings of kindness, compassion and empathy with at least one family member? Did they give any examples of kindness, compassion, and empathy?

Page 44 - kindness, compassion, gratitude, empathy

Page 45 - Share your Gratitude List with someone.

Page 46 - Be kind to animals.

Page 47 - Rise and shine.

Page 48 - B.

Page 50 - 1 c, 2 b, 3 c, 4 d, 5 a, 6 c, 7 b

Page 51 - 8 b, 9 c, 10 b, 11 c, 12 c, 13 d, 14 d, 15 b

Page 52 - 1 T, 2 F, 3 F, 4 F, 5 T, 6 F, 7 T, 8 T, 9 F, 10 F
collar, tag, guardian's information on tag, microchip.
love

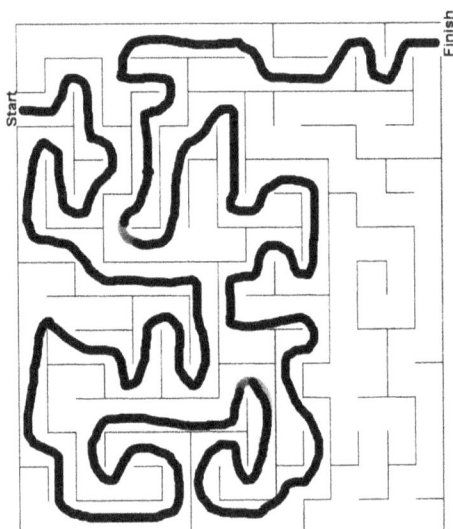

Page 41

Page 49

Sweeetie Certificate

Sweeetie

This certifies that

_____

has successfully completed
"The Sweeet Old Lady Coloring and Activity Book"
and is an Official "Sweeetie."

This "Sweeetie" has learned about
kindness, compassion, empathy and gratitude
and the importance of cats and dogs having microchips
and wearing collars and tags that
identify their guardian.

_____
Signature of an adult

Date _____

The Sweeet Old Lady Down the Street

Score

Catherine D. Killam

Allegro)211-08= ♩ (

C   C/G

Voice

There's   a   sweeet   old   la - dy down   the

F   C/G   G   C

street.   Down the street.   She's the   kind of   la - dy you should   meet. You should   meet. Her   face

G   C   F

is   full   of   wrink - les.   Her   eye's   are   full   of   twink -

Dm   C   G   C

les.   She's the   sweeet   old   la - dy down   the   street.   Down   the   street.

"The Sweeet Old Lady Down the Street Song" may be heard and viewed with American Sign Language at "The Sweeet Old Lady" - YouTube, "The Sweeet Old Lady" Facebook page, and enchantedforestpublishing.com.

2. There's a sweeet old lady down the street.
Down the street.
She's the kind of lady you should meet.
You should meet.
Her voice is full of glee
and she'd never harm a flea
She's the sweeet old lady down the street.
Down the street.

3. There's a sweeet old lady down the street.
Down the street.
She's the kind of lady you should meet.
You should meet.
She wears purple dresses
and flowers in her tresses.
She's the sweeet old lady down the street.
Down the street.

4. There's a sweeet old lady down the street.
Down the street.
She's the kind of lady you should meet.
You should meet.
She wears funky shoes
and crazy hairdos.
She's the sweeet old lady down the street.
Down the street.

5. There's a sweeet old lady down the street.
Down the street.
She's the kind of lady you should meet.
You should meet.
She feeds cats and dogs
and little green frogs.
She's the sweeet old lady down the street.
Down the street.

6. There's a sweeet old lady down the street.
Down the street.
She's the kind of lady you should meet.
You should meet.
She has fairies in her yard
and she talks like a bard.
She's the sweeet old lady down the street.
Down the street.

7. There's a sweeet old lady down the street.
Down the street.
She's the kind of lady you should meet.
You should meet.
She drinks herbal teas
under a canopy of trees.
There's a sweeet old lady down the street.
Down the street.

8. There's a sweeet old lady down the street.
Down the street.
She's the kind of lady you should meet.
You should meet.
She makes a soup of nettle
in a large copper kettle.
There's a sweeet old lady down the street.
Down the street.

9. There's a sweeet old lady down the street.
Down the street.
She's the kind of lady you should meet.
You should meet.
She dances under the moon
to her favorite tune.
She's the sweeet old lady down the street.
Down the street.

10. There's a sweeet old lady down the street.
Down the street.
She's the kind of lady you should meet.
You should meet.
She dances with bats
and wears earrings of cats.
She's the sweeet old lady down the street.
Down the street.

11. There's a sweeet old lady down the street.
Down the street.
She's the kind of lady you should meet.
You should meet.
Her cupboard is full of herbs
and she heals with words.
She's the sweeet old lady down the street.
Down the street.

12. There's a sweeet old lady down the street.
Down the street.
She's the kind of lady you should meet.
You should meet.
She makes tasty dishes
filled with love and special wishes.
She's the sweeet old lady down the street.
Down the street.

Further information about words or phrases used in the book.

Blessed be: The phrase "blessed be" is found in some modern spiritual paths. It's a saying that means that a person wishes another person positive things.

Do no harm: Is a central tenet of the Hippocratic Oath that is taken by physicians. "Harm none, do what thou wilt." is a tenet of some earth-based spiritual paths. It is a concept and guidance for right living.

Funny-looking cards: Refers to Tarot cards which is a set of 78 cards used for meditation, affirmations, insight, and the study of archetypal symbols. It represents the journey of the Fool (the spirit) through life and all the things that are learned and understood along the way, such as challenges faced and ways of overcoming them. It is included in this book to help educate some people who may have negative associations regarding the cards.

Healing arts: The author's definition of some healing arts are: Reiki, Healing Touch, Therapeutic Touch, energy work, massage, acupressure, flower and gem essences, etc.

Lavender: Is a flowering plant. It is grown mainly to make an essential oil which has antiseptic and anti-inflammatory properties. It is also used as a fragrance for bath and food products.

Kitty loving time: Is a special time at the author's cat sanctuary when she calls out to the cats and they come running to her for affection, grooming and treats.

Microchip: It is a chip about the size of a grain of rice that is inserted under the skin on the back of the neck of a dog or cat by a veterinarian. It has a special number that is assigned to the pet's guardian such as their name, address, and phone number. That information is registered with the company from whom the chip was purchased, the pet's veterinarian or the local humane society. The information needs to be updated whenever the pet's guardian moves, changes their phone number or places the pet in another home.

Natal chart: It is a horoscope/astrological chart drawn for the exact time of an individual's birth at a particular place on Earth for the purposes of gaining information about the individual.

Nettle soup: Is a traditional soup prepared from stinging nettles. There are many health benefits associated with the stinging nettle.

Rose hip oil: Is the fruit of the rose plant. It has many benefits to help the skin.

Strawberry moon: Naming full moons dates back to the Native Americans tribes. The tribes kept track of the season by giving distinctive names to each recurring full moon. Strawberries were harvested in June so the full moon that occurs during June was named for the strawberry.

Sweeet: Author's Definition - An older woman who is enchanting, charming, colorful, creative, compassionate, kind, strong, courageous and bold. She embraces and celebrates life to its fullest. She doesn't let anyone tell her what to do. She is true to herself.

Tag: Is a metal label attached to a pet's collar with the name of the pet's guardian and phone number.

Three-fold law or Law of return: Is a tenet held by some spiritual paths that believe that whatever energy a person puts out into the world, be it positive or negative, will be returned to that person three times.

About the Author: Catherine D. Killam, also known as "Cat"

From her beginnings in the San Francisco Bay Area to living around the world in such places as Guam, Scotland and Oahu, Catherine and her husband settled on the Big Island of Hawaii. Catherine enjoyed her years of being a military wife, having her own paralegal business, hypnotherapy and massage practice, and flower and gem essence business.

She found her passion in rescuing stray and abandoned cats and providing them a safe place to live. She and her husband founded Cat-Care, a 501(c)3 nonprofit in 1998. They have rescued well over 500 animals either through reuniting them with their owners or providing temporary or permanent shelter. The residents of "The Cat House" are spayed or neutered and receive veterinary care. The Killams have also prevented thousands of unwanted cats from being born by rescuing cats from their dump and having the cats spayed or neutered.

With the recent addition of twin granddaughters, a new passion has been awakened in Catherine. While reading to her granddaughters she noticed a lack of positive role models for older women. It seemed like the only books about older woman had them living in a shoe, having bare cupboards, swallowing a fly, snow, etc., or being cruel to children. After singing, "This old man ..." one too many times, she wanted to sing a song about an old lady. Thus the Sweeet Old Lady was born. It started with a song and ended with this book. Part of the book is a blending of fact and fiction. The Killams do live in an enchanted forest surrounded by tall trees. They live in a red and white gingerbread house and have fed lots of dogs. They have a separate house just for cats. However, The Sweeet Old Lady is the woman Catherine wishes to become. Many times throughout the day, she'll ask herself if she is being the Sweeet Old Lady or not. When situations arise, she also asks herself, "What would the Sweeet Old Lady do?" Maybe you might begin asking yourself that same question.

In addition to wanting a book to depict an elderly woman in a positive light, Catherine also wanted to increase awareness on ways to further help animals. She feels that it is important to educate children about responsible pet ownership. She has taught over 80 humane education classes. In her experience in rescuing animals over the last 14 years, she knows that guardian identification is the single most important thing a pet guardian can do to assist their pets in being returned. A section on life saving tips for pets will be included in all her children's books.

"The Sweeet Old Lady Down the Street" can be used as part of a humane education program. It can be read aloud to elementary school students and the Coloring and Activity Book can supplement activities.

"The Sweeet Old Lady Coloring and Activity Book" The book includes pages to color, puzzles, a maze, quiz questions, etc. There are also review questions designed to assist in reading retention of the main book. The books can be used together in a home schooling situation. Individual sheets can be copied and used as part of the humane education program, home schooling or family activity.

"The Sweeet Old Lady Down the Street Song" may be heard and viewed with American Sign Language on "The Sweeet Old Lady" - You Tube, "The Sweeet Old Lady" Facebook page, and enchantedforestpublishing.com. If you wish to connect with Catherine please visit her Page on Facebook, "The Sweeet Old Lady." You may also email her at sweeetoldlady@gmail.com or enchantedforestpublishing@gmail.com..

About the Illustrator: Richard Svensson

Richard lives in Sweden and pursues a career as an illustrator. His work has been featured on Swedish and Norwegian television, and in a selection of international magazines, books and comics.

Life Saving Tips for your pets.

The most important thing you can do to ensure your pet will be returned to you, should they ever get lost, is to have a collar with a tag and your name and phone number on it. If possible, also write your phone number on your pet's collar. It is not necessary to have your pet's name on the tag. It is your name that is important. Just having a collar is not enough. All a collar means is that your pet does have a home. Thousands of dogs and cats with collars end up at the humane society and, unfortunately, most are not reunited with their owners. Please have your pet spayed or neutered to prevent pet overpopulation which leads to many unwanted animals.

Please make sure your pets are micro-chipped. That is important should they ever lose their collar. Simply having a microchip is not enough either. Kind-hearted people take in animals not knowing they have a microchip. Be sure you have registered the microchip number along with your name and phone number with your local humane society, veterinarian and company who issued the microchip. Remember to update your information should you move, change your phone number or your pet gets a new guardian. A collar and a tag will make it easy for anyone who finds your pet to easily call you and to return your beloved pet to you. Should your pet end up at the humane society, the microchip will help them reunite you and your pet.

Some food and products that may be dangerous to your pet.

According to the Pet Poison Helpline, The Humane Society of the United States, Doctors Foster and Smith Pet Education, the following foods and products may be dangerous to your pet: alcohol, apricot pits, avocado, caffeine, cherry pits, chocolate, garlic, grapes, hops, macadamia nuts, moldy food, mushrooms, onions, peach pits, raisins, salt, star fruit, yeast dough, xylitol (sugar substitute that is used in sugar free gum).

Some other items that may also be dangerous to your pet: anthurium, antifreeze, fertilizers, gasoline, glow sticks, hornets, kerosene, lilies, pesticides, mouse and rat poison, tea tree oil, poinsettia, spiders, toads, vitamins, and windshield wiper fluid.

Please visit their websites for a full list of food and products or consult your veterinarian. www.petpoisonhelpline.com, www.humanesociety.org/animals/resources/.../foods_poisonous_to_pets, www.peteducation.com. Look for foods to Avoid Feeding Your Cat and Foods to Avoid Feeding Your Dog.

There have been many pet food and pet treat recalls. Please check the below listed websites periodically to see if any of your pet's food or treats have been the subject of an alert or recall. http://www.fda.gov/animalVeterinary/safetyhealth/recallswithdrawals/default.htm https://www.avma.org/news/issues/recalls-alerts/pages/pet-food-safety-recalls-alerts.aspx

The author is not affiliated with any of the above-listed websites.

www.ingramcontent.com/pod-product-compliance
Lightning Source LLC
Chambersburg PA
CBHW080531030426
42337CB00023B/4693